FINDING THE POINT OF EQUILIBRIUM

SCHIZOAFFECTIVE DISORDER AND WELL-BEING, LIVING THE PARADOX

Beatrice Walsh

Gotham Books

30 N Gould St.
Ste. 20820, Sheridan, WY 82801

Phone: 1 (307) 464-7800

© 2023 *Beatrice Walsh*. All rights reserved.

No part of this book may be reproduced, stored in a retrieval system, or transmitted by any means without the written permission of the author.

Published by Gotham Books (September 14, 2023)

ISBN: 979-8-88775-509-0 (P)
ISBN: 979-8-88775-510-6 (E)

Because of the dynamic nature of the Internet, any web addresses or links contained in this book may have changed since publication and may no longer be valid.

The views expressed in this work are solely those of the author and do not necessarily reflect the views of the publisher, and the publisher hereby disclaims any responsibility for them.

1ST PART

1. BREAKDOWN

"Beatrice, you are late, come to the office I (manager) and Brian (general manager) want to talk to you "............. Sounds serious I thought, since when is it a crime to be late for work?

"We are very concerned about you; you have been late a lot recently and you have been very unhappy. This is not like you. Something is wrong. We think you need a break. We called your husband; he is coming to pick you up and take you home".

.... ???......!!!!!.........??...

Hold your horses. This is coming out of the blue. What is happening? ...."Did I do something wrong?"

"No, you didn't do anything wrong. You are and have been very late and your husband says you leave home on time. Why are you so late? What have you been doing?"

(After a long while)

What have you been doing????........................

We are very concerned about you. ....

"Beatrice, something is not right with you, maybe something with your heart".

"Nothing's wrong with me".

"Please wait for your husband, he will take you home. Do you want someone to stay with you?"

"Yes, I do Mariya – a colleague and a friend".

I didn't say it but, in fact, as well as my job at the nursery, I worked with an anti-terrorist network. While driving to work I had been followed and I had to lose them. I drove around through little streets and waited; only when I was satisfied, they were gone, did I continue on my way to work.

It's just that I work for the police as well as my job here. I have the ability to see how things connect and interact; this allows me to predict what will happen next.

But now I'm here at the nursery and my bosses don't even want me to work this morning. Yet we are busy. I'm good at my job, I know I am. My managers are ok too, but they want my husband to take me home. What on earth is going on? This is not happening. How can they tell me there is something not right and cannot say what is wrong….. and why do I feel so tense, so shattered, so lost all of a sudden……..

I became agitated, pacing up and down, talking and gesturing to Mariya, who would gently tell me not to take everything so intensely.

I felt bewildered, furious, anxious, scared……..

When my husband Shaune came and we drove out of the car park and I saw my car there, the same car that I had driven to work that morning, something tilted.

I was still furious but, at the same time, doubts started invading my mind. I oscillated between fury and terror. Fury at my bosses for dismissing me, terror that I was going crazy. Once home I went to bed – got up – didn't want to talk – talked saying the same things over and over again – sat down – paced the floor – and again, and again. Shaune tried to calm me. He said, "We'll just go to the doctor and take it from there".

An explosion took place in my head. My thoughts scattered in all directions. I didn't know what to do with myself or with anything else for that matter. The next day Shaune took me to see my GP, who organised for me to see a psychiatrist the following day.

I went on believing that the whole mess would be cleared up. I could explain my job with the anti-terrorist unit and the psychiatrist would then talk to Shaune and my workplace and I could just continue on as before!

SOMEHOW IT DIDN'T TURN OUT THAT WAY!

I sat there, face to face with the psychiatrist and told him my story: I was married, we had three children. I was working in a plant nursery part time, but my real job was to assist the anti-terrorist police as a "consultant". It was dangerous and for safety reasons I didn't talk about it with anyone. (I suspected that my house and my phone had been bugged). We communicated through codes placed in newspapers, on radio and television.

He listened very attentively and asked me some questions "How are you getting paid for this work?" I had no answer; there was a lot I couldn't answer. He set out explaining what was happening to me. "You don't know what's real and what's not real. It's called psychosis. Have you seen the movie "A Beautiful Mind?" I had. "But my children are growing up"?! "I'm not saying your children are not real".

So, what was real, what was not? I wasn't sure. I wasn't sure of anything anymore, least of all of who I was.

He prescribed medication. I am and I have always been against taking drugs of any kind. I didn't consider myself ill, but he encouraged me to take it, saying I really needed it. I ended up taking it.

For about another month I was living in a world of anti-terrorism networks, code cracking, plots and counter plots, people following me, receiving instructions, and sometimes acting, sending secret signals to perceived colleagues, at times believing I, or my family, were in terrible danger. It was frightening but also exciting; a bit unreal as if I was in another dimension, separate from others.

At the same time, I was also a wife, a mum, a worker, and the patient of a psychiatrist. At those times I felt humiliated and totally confused.

After about a month "it", all the ideas in my head, the not real happenings, disappeared, and there I was, the "old" me: boring, not too smart, hypersensitive, at the mercy of all the emotions and stresses, good and bad, in and around me and to top it all, I now knew that I had lost my mind and with that any emotional and mental confidence I had possessed before.

(It was not going to be so easy as I had several relapses, each time quite different, and I was totally unable to distinguish what was real, what was not. To me it was all absolutely real.)

2. SPIRALLING DOWN

I was unable to function at home nor at work!

The ground under my feet had tilted – I was going downhill. I hadn't been able to sleep well for a long time, but it got even worse. I was up several times for long periods each night, woke up really early and it was impossible to get back to sleep; but getting up to start the day demanded a gigantic effort. Everything became so difficult. I was carrying a mountain on my shoulders; it made me so terribly tired all the time. I often went back to bed; it was all just too heavy; when I tried to get up again, I felt even worse.

Then I lost my footing altogether, I was in a whirl – being swept up by the turmoil in me. Thoughts raced around in my head, perceived short-comings at work became an obsession. I would think about the same things over and over again, talk about the issue non-stop with my husband and some friends, get all worked up and very anxious. I just couldn't switch off. Every complex, every fear, every hurt that I had experienced throughout my life and up until now, blew out of all proportion, out of all reason. I couldn't function, couldn't concentrate, even the simplest tasks were out of reach, impossible to do. Thoughts of killing myself kept springing up in my mind. I was drowning, I sensed it physically. I was drowning or spiralling down inside a bottomless well, both sensations. I was suffocating, I couldn't breathe. The world had shrunk to just me and my despair. The only way to stop this was to kill myself, there was no other way, living had become too hard – I just couldn't do it.

And yet, very very fleetingly at first, I remembered that I used to say and think that I would never knowingly hurt my children. I meant it and I still do. Deep down I knew that me committing suicide would definitely hurt them and all those around me. I knew because a friend of mine had done it and I had seen and felt some of the devastation it had caused.

The conflict between wanting to live and to stop living was unbearable. The only relief I felt was when I was with someone. Someone else's presence gave me a little bit of strength, allowing me to continue living a bit longer.

By now I was taking antidepressants, seeing my psychiatrist regularly and still falling deeper and deeper into the well.

I was empty, exhausted, had no strength, mental nor physical, left. Sadness, like a river of mud, the river of my thoughts, heavy, obsessive, gloomy, engulfed me and there was no one to help me – I was alone.

The reality was that, in fact, I had a loving husband and children, family and friends, doctors. Everyone desperately trying to help, but I felt separate, disconnected, and numb.

I finally hit the bottom of the well. High walls surrounded me. I was shut off, out of reach, unable to connect with the outside world. I was so scared I felt sick. Scared that I would never be able to function again, scared that I would always be dependent, scared that I would never be able to work again, terrified of being lonely forever. I was a prisoner of my thoughts and feelings.

At the same time, deep down, I wanted and yearned for interaction with the people around me, especially with my family. My heart ached, everything ached. I didn't understand why this was happening, why did I feel so desperately unhappy?

I agreed to go into a psychiatric hospital.

I only stayed in hospital for two weeks. At the time I didn't think it helped that much. It did give me a bit of respite though: I was not alone, there were other people struggling. Also, being observed, I wasn't going to kill myself because I wouldn't succeed, I would be rescued, so that battle receded a bit, for all the wrong reasons but still, it gave me a kind of a break. I had a session three times a week with my psychiatrist. His diagnosis was melancholic depression.

As well as that, no matter how down and miserable I felt, my husband and my children were there. They visited every day and we just sat together. I was not able to hold a real conversation, I was withdrawn; I realised it, but I couldn't do anything about it, I didn't know how.

My family (brother, sisters, and mother) lived in Switzerland and called regularly giving me lots of support. I missed them, I was so homesick and this in itself was an illness. My sisters wanted to drop everything and come, but I told them not to. Somehow, I realised that I had to be able to live my normal life again. My life was here with my husband and children. I realised I needed to get better here in my ordinary life.

"What's changed?" My doctor asked when I demanded to go back home to a very similar situation as before: still unable to function, very depressed and to an empty house during weekdays.

However, the turmoil in my head had slowed down somewhat and little gaps, like pools of clear water in the river of my thoughts, appeared and at those times I could "think", squeeze in a thought coming from myself, the me that could feel, that could sense. These gaps were brief – few and far between – and I hardly noticed them, so caught up was I in the "other" thinking: worries, obsessive cycles of negative thinking, ruminations, feelings of unworthiness, fear, and anxiety.

Being by myself while my husband and children were at work or studying was still a danger, for left on my own, those distressing thoughts and feelings would take over again. I had no power to stop them. It's not that I didn't want to get better. By now I understood that I had an illness and I really wanted to get better. I was hurting and so too were the people who loved me. I could see that.

I had told some friends how terrible I felt when I was on my own. So, Debbie organised a little roster with Barbara, Trish, and Lauraine, so that someone would visit regularly, or we would meet over coffee. Di, who lived further away and worked full time, phoned regularly and we socialised on the weekends. Sue invited us to join a group she belonged to. Trish and Barbara came walking with me regularly, my Swiss family phoned every day. I also saw my doctor every week, so I did have some things in place to hold me. All these acts of kindness were my lifelines.

I also encountered the "get yourself together, you've nothing to complain about" attitudes and to some extent, these remarks were true, too. I was physically healthy and seemed to have everything needed to be happy, but I wasn't. I told myself many times I should be happy, I should be doing this and that, at least keep the house clean, do the shopping and cooking, but I couldn't. I could go to the supermarket, but once there I was not capable of buying food for dinner, for example; I didn't know what to buy nor how.

I still felt empty and numb. The days dragged on and on; I will never complain again that time goes too fast. Time nearly stopped then, and it's not a good feeling.

3. CHILDHOOD YEARS.

Up until my illness, I had lived a fairly normal life. I grew up in Fribourg, Switzerland and had a reasonably happy childhood. My father died when I and my twin sister were two, so my mother found herself a widow with four kids under six: an older brother, an older sister and us. My father had a small business, a leather goods shop and upholstery workshop. My mother took it over so she could provide for us. We lived above the business and my paternal grandmother and aunt also lived in the same house but in a different flat.

There was a lot of conflict between my mother, paternal grandmother, and aunt. Instead of being supportive of my mother, they were critical and also tried to control our upbringing. My first memory of my childhood is seeing my mother crying on an armchair in her bedroom. There was also lots of love: my mother loved us with all her might, which was considerable, she had a strong personality. My grandmother died when I was young and eventually my aunt moved out, not so gracefully. My maternal grandmother also died when I was young. I have good memories of her and remember playing shop on her balcony.

Christiane (my twin) and I played a lot. We had more freedom than most since my mother worked long hours as well as looking after us. Our house was full of nooks and crannies to play in. As we got a bit older, we just had to be home for lunch and by dinnertime. We would ride our scooters for hours, play with the local kids in the street, and go to the park, the swimming pool in summer, the ice rink in winter and tobogganing in winter as well. It was quite safe; we were all over town exploring and having a great time. The downside of all this freedom is that sometimes, we lacked guidance, no one to "explain" things, no one to show us the ways of the world.

At five I started preschool. My preschool was run by nuns. There was only one class per year. Sister Octavie was my first-year teacher, and Sister Elizabeth my second-year teacher.

Sister Octavie was quite old and had years of experience teaching preschool children. She was highly regarded and respected. I didn't like her much, she believed in discipline and there were many times during the day when we were not allowed to talk; I had a fair bit of trouble with that. In the teacher/parent interview she told my mother that I was not too bright and that I would always have difficulties learning. When in subsequent years I did have those difficulties: my marks were low, spelling my bête noire, math not much better, my mother would say "Sister Octavie was right". My mother didn't do everything right.

Fribourg, my hometown, is a Catholic stronghold. My family was Catholic and nearly everyone I knew was too.

Everyone went to church, and we also had religious education at school. I was taught about a God who is everywhere and watches you always (you couldn't even fart without God knowing it). Sins were big and we had compulsory confession. I wanted to be good so that my mother and God would be happy and sometimes I believed I had been very good. But, as I was told many times, we are all sinners and no one is perfect, only God and Jesus are perfect. We are even born with a mortal sin, and we'd better be good (even though we could never be good enough) and repent our "sins" because when we die God will judge us and send us to purgatory or heaven or hell. There seemed to be a lot of emphasis on punishment. At the same time, we were told that God is love but how this translated into love for me was not clear.

Luckily, at home, religion was not pushed hard on us kids. However, we didn't discuss it either and it would have been considered quite improper to question teachers and priests. Another thing that was never discussed was sex.

My mother never remarried. No man had any role in my upbringing apart from the priests at church and they were remote, thank God!

My twin and I belonged to the Brownies. We had music lessons and belonged to a children's choir all of which were run by women. My teachers were women.

Two men worked in my mum's workshop; we lived upstairs. At noon they would go home for lunch, lunch being the main meal of the day. The shop was closed from noon until 1:30pm. We had lunch ourselves and my mum would stay upstairs for a while to tidy up and do some other chores. Often, one of the men, Didi, was first back. He would ring the bell and my mum would send one of us downstairs to open the door and let him in.

It is at those times that Didi would call me to him and under the pretext of playing with me, he would fondle my barely emerging breasts again and again, so hard that it hurt. This happened many times over a long period. I didn't know what was happening. I didn't tell anyone.

I tried to not go and open the door, but disobeying my mum was not on. Disobeying adults in general was not on. We were taught about stranger danger but never explicitly what that danger was and anyway Didi was not a stranger.

Eventually I grew to the age when we talk about boys with school friends, and we had anatomy lessons at high school and also, I could read about it. I would simply evade Didi and put his advances out of my mind. After all, I hadn't been "raped".

But "it" did not go out of my mind. It's in my heart and guts, buried in the deepest part of my mind and in every cell of my body.

So, at 15 my school years ended. I had been struggling all through them. Because I wasn't a good student and also because I was a bit unruly, I was often criticized by my teachers. These remarks were usually derogatory: not trying hard enough, my work not good enough, being lazy. I felt all of these criticisms very strongly. I was hardly ever praised.

At home with my mother and my siblings we had our ups and downs. It mustn't have been easy for my mum to care and provide for all of us, while managing the business and the house. Two of her sisters helped occasionally but she was mainly doing it on her own. Money was tight adding to her worries. Like all kids we were quite messy. When it got too much she would explode and we would move – I mean move – and in no time the house was tidy again, for a little while! I don't advocate this method though; there was quite a bit of anger in it, but it would pass quickly.

There were lots of good times too. My mum liked having the family over and she still had the energy to gather everyone on many occasions. She loved singing, and every time, after a glass of wine, she would start singing and everyone joined in. We sang folksongs, as Fribourg is rich in song traditions. Also, we often went on walks in the mountains, the forest or the countryside nearby, on picnics, etc., etc. I loved being outside in nature, I still do.

At 15 I started an apprenticeship in horticulture in my town's botanical gardens. I loved being amongst trees and flowers and plants, I enjoyed the work. My boss was quite strict, but he was very knowledgeable and happy to teach the apprentices. At Technical College, I was interested in what I was taught; I did well.

So, there I was: a young adult. I dreamed of travelling, seeing the world. I didn't want to do it on my own.

A colleague of mine had been in Israel as a volunteer in a kibbutz. It had been a great experience for her, and she spoke enthusiastically about it. At the time I was working in an alpine botanical garden. It was only open in summer as it was covered in snow in winter. I wished to return the following year, so I decided I too would go to work in a kibbutz as a volunteer. It was a common thing to do for young people at the time. I registered with an office and off I went to Kibbutz

Guinnosar and that is where I met the man who was going to be my husband. He was from Sydney. I didn't know much about Australia at the time, and I didn't speak English, but we managed to communicate, and we fell in love.

I came to Australia one and a half years later (it was a big decision). We got married and we had three children. We lived an "ordinary" life in the suburbs. And we lived happily ever after... or so, this is how it was supposed to be.

But now in my late 40's I am at the bottom of a deep well, terrified, sad; my mind and my body unable to function, feeling useless, incredibly lonely. I had no energy to the point that even going to the letter box at the front of my home was an effort. I had always enjoyed good food, but now I had to make myself eat because I knew that to live you have to eat. My heart was full of dread.

There seemed to be no reason why I should feel like that, it didn't make sense. But I did and that was very real.

So, what went wrong?

4. SCHIZO-AFFECTIVE DISORDER

The diagnosis was now schizo-affective disorder.

Time went by, and with all the care and the medication helping, I didn't have this overwhelming desire to kill myself anymore and I was sort of functioning, but I was still lifeless and sad. Everything was so difficult: from getting up in the morning to going to bed at night. At least I could sleep now; I think the medication helped there.

After a few months I decided to go back to work. Work gave me a structure. It gave me a sense of belonging, belonging to society, being useful. I worked three days a week; it created a rhythm to go by, an anchor that offered stability.

At the same time work was also a source of stress. We were often short-staffed, and I felt that the way things were organised was not always helpful. Dealing with the public was often not easy.

My psychiatrist suggested that we start psychotherapy, to which I agreed.

This ended up being one of the most helpful things I ever did. It was not me talking all the time and my doctor just listening, it was more like a guided search for answers, a search to understand what happened and what was still happening in my life.

Often, I didn't know what to say. I was closed; it was very difficult to express myself. I found it quite confronting to open up to somebody else about my deepest feelings and thoughts. So confronting in fact, that I never mentioned the abuse. I had not forgotten, but I couldn't talk about it; I was frightened and distrustful of anyone I perceived as having some "authority" over me and, mostly, I dismissed it as not being important since I hadn't been "raped".

Even though I didn't fully open up, the psychotherapy helped. I started feeling better and I was making progress towards wellbeing. Eventually I stopped taking medication and I was doing quite well: being able to do what needed doing, living a "normal" life. It was not all plain sailing – at times I was still anxious, depressed, and sad for no obvious reason. But we all have ups and downs – that's life. After all, aren't we told that "life wasn't meant to be easy".

My doctor announced that he was going to leave in three months. We had developed a good doctor/patient relationship, and I felt that the regular visits helped me a lot. I was regaining confidence and life was quite good. It was getting towards the time when I could stand on my own two feet without needing to go and see a psychiatrist. I was also quite active in trying to promote my own wellbeing and the wellbeing of others around me.

I exercised regularly (fundamental to wellbeing), ate a balanced diet, lots of fresh food that I cooked for myself and my family. I was back at work part time, drank in moderation, and I had interests outside work too. My husband and I are keen bushwalkers and I also love to read and enjoyed my garden again. I also had lots of support from family and friends.

So, I had good reasons to be optimistic.

But "The heart has its reasons of which reason knows nothing… " (Blaise Pascal) a favourite saying of my mum, who had an innate wisdom. I was fine for a while and then I started slipping into the downward spiral again. This time I knew what was happening and I took anti-depressants straight away, to no avail.

Work was stressful, that hadn't changed. At the same time, I liked working and I liked the people with whom I worked, and it gave me the structure that I needed. But I know now that stress is a killer, especially when one has a mental vulnerability, a frailty. Some of the stress was coming from outside, but a lot was the effect and result of my own (mistaken) beliefs, creating a vicious circle in which I generated even more stress to the point that anxiety and panic invaded my mind again, taking over despite all my will power and effort. I was unable to function again. I sunk into despair; I had been trying so very hard to get well and to stay well. It seemed totally hopeless. Again, strong impulses of killing myself filled up my head and my heart. I couldn't think of anything else. (This happens spontaneously, automatically, sort of despite myself, I had no input into these ideas of suicide.)   Again, I didn't do it!

So, the only other thing I could do was going back to see a psychiatrist, back to hospital. I felt utterly defeated.

I was so exhausted, so down I couldn't even speak properly. The words didn't come to my mind – I couldn't find them. This didn't happen with everyone, just to make it even more confusing.

I was back to square one.

So, I started again with a new doctor, not easy. At first, I was so sure that the situation was hopeless and that nothing could help that I was a very reluctant patient, and I still didn't trust anyone with "authority" over me. But I was desperate, so I went along.

Several years down the track my doctor has been and is an excellent, kind, and caring doctor for me. I am very grateful for the help both doctors have given me. They both played a pivotal role in my recovery.

After a second stay in hospital and with medication I could function again and I was reasonably happy, back living a good, normal life.

However, there were still times when I felt that terrible sense of emptiness, especially when on my own and times when I felt really melancholic and sad, as well as times of strong anxiety; I still experienced panic attacks. I could get "over it" now but I felt it limited what I could do enormously.

2ND *PART*

1. SEARCHING FOR A NEW WAY

I became curious about my condition. I have observed many times people who suffered a heart attack or a stroke, or people with cancer, finding out as much as they can about their present condition, as well as going to the doctor, and making changes in their lifestyle in order to help their recovery and (when it works out that way), sticking to that, in order to stay healthy.

I too suffered and even though no x-ray or MRI or blood test would show it, the pain was none the less very real. I felt it and my family and friends felt it. Some of the time I was still hurting inside, and I was also hurting my husband and children. Everyone was subdued, I could see that.

The situation was rather puzzling. I knew my husband and children loved me and I loved them, our home was harmonious, and I could function quite well again.

In fact, like most people, I had been, I still am a "good" person trying to do the "right thing".

However, there was room for improvement! And I felt a very strong desire to be as healthy as I can (don't we all), for myself, but also for my family who had given me so much support.

For me, being healthy meant being fit, feeling good physically, emotionally, and spiritually, and being free of medication, in a broad sense, all medication: natural health supplements included, alcohol, sugar, anything we consume to make ourselves feel better.

Basically, being happy and well.

The question is how? Do I? Can I?

Is it realistic? Am I asking too much? Should I be contented with the present situation?

I was grateful for all the progress I had made and was still making. Every step of the way had required the skills and care of my doctors, the support of my family and friends and support at work. At the same time, it had also required a tenacious effort on my part.

For example, when I say I exercised regularly, it sounds easy, simple. We all know that exercising is good for you. It's just a matter of choice, of willpower and discipline we are told, so just do it, as the ad says.

Well, all this is true, but it is not the complete truth, the reality.

My reality ***at the depths of my illness*** was that I was extremely fatigued, and thoughts spun uncontrollably fast in my head all the time. The effect of this made me unable to function, unable to think above this mind tsunami, unable to make a decision, unable to remember anything else, unable to move, literally and metaphorically; so, setting goals and sticking to them was unreachable from where I stood then.

At this point I really needed medication. I recognised that I must take it so that I can get better, so that I can function again. However, I was determined to stop taking it as soon as possible. It did help though. It slowed my thinking down and also helped lift that heavy weight off my shoulders that made everything impossibly hard to do. It enabled me to rest to some degree, so I recovered a tiny bit of energy.

However, it didn't magically make me well and happy,

>It didn't magically make me full of energy.
>
>It didn't magically clear my mind.
>
>It didn't magically make me feel good.
>
>It didn't initiate action for me.
>
>It didn't make decisions for me.

And most importantly, it didn't change my deep sense that I am just not good enough, not intelligent enough, therefore others are better than me, are smarter than me (inferiority complex), therefore I don't really matter : **me being here is irrelevant.** At the level of my head, I thought that I was basically all right and I was living a good life, trying to do my best. But at the level of the emotional heart (in the dimension of the spirit) I didn't know THIS.

This I was going to have to find out and do myself, in conjunction with the treatment and with the support of others.

The question was how?

How can I recover that positive spark that makes it possible to initiate something, to trigger a new thinking mechanism, to take that first step in a new direction towards wellbeing? And then to keep going?

Now that not all of my thinking was taken by the idea of killing myself, I felt a strong desire (will) to live and to feel good and be happy (normal state of being)

We all have this desire within ourselves, and it is this desire that pushes us forward (Aristotle)

By the way, I often ask myself where does this desire come from?

How come I had lost it and now I had it back?

I believe that the medication helped but I also believe that it was a "miracle" as well. I couldn't help thinking that somehow God had something to do with it.

I wanted to get better so much that it pushed me to do something about it. I decided I would start with exercising again, but it was bloody difficult. At first, I couldn't do it on my own; there again, I needed help. I was dependent on others' help for all my doings. I had always been fiercely independent, so this state of affairs pained me a lot.

I needed to regain the ability to act on my own. I needed to find a way forward (at the time it was just intuition – I sensed this).

I had read about overcoming resistance, so I set myself a precise starting time, in the morning, after breakfast , but before everything else, not if I felt like it or not, or if I had the time, or if I was not too tired. That time space after breakfast was "sacred". No excuse, especially the Big One we all use all the time: I am too busy! After all, we were five people at home and I wanted to be useful. (Even though, then, I couldn't do anything)   Resist the temptation to just sit down or lie down.

I also knew I needed to start small because "how can we take big steps before we take little steps?" (Thich Nhat Hanh). We can't, no one can.

I encouraged myself: 10 minutes I would say to myself, it's OK, I can do it. Sometimes even this was too hard so I would reduce it to three minutes. ***<u>The most important thing was to start</u>.*** I put music on to carry me along; I love music, beautiful music and loud because it seemed to penetrate into my brain, and with a fast beat because I sensed that my heart, emotional and physical, my brain, my body and my mind needed a bit of a shake to push them into action, shake them out of the numbness and put a bit of life into them: into me.

And it did just that, I felt better afterwards, momentarily, but still this was progress – a small step in the right direction.

Some days I couldn't shake myself, never mind, tomorrow is a new day, a new beginning, a new step, try again and again and I did, enough of the time. In turn, slowly my energy increased, and it became easier, I felt lighter so I could do more and I did more and so on.

Slowly, step by step, I was rebuilding some strength: emotionally: my mood lifted, physically: it generated energy, mentally: my brain functioned a bit better after exercise, but also spiritually because of the fact that I (myself) was actually able to do something towards feeling better. I had found a minute amount of power over the illness: a real monster in me; the infamous black dog crushing me down and barking incessantly at me from within and driving me crazy. Actually,

I now think that 'black dog' is much too gentle a metaphor for what I experienced. I found a much more accurate description in J.K. Rowling's dementors:

"Dementors are among the foulest creatures that walk the earth. They infest the darkest, filthiest places, they glory in decay and despair, they drain peace, hope, and happiness out of the air around them….Get too near a dementor and every good feeling, every happy memory will be sucked out of you. If it can, the dementor will feed on you long enough to reduce you to something like itself…soulless and evil. You will be left with nothing but the worst experiences of your life."

With the major difference that my dementors live inside me!!

Nonetheless (back to exercising) these moments of feeling OK motivated me to persist.

In conjunction with the care, support, and medicine I was receiving I had found a strategy to activate myself: mentally, emotionally, physically and spiritually, because all these are linked, inter-connected, and when you activate one you activate the other.

So, it seemed to me that I had found a tiny door opening onto a path out of the vicious cycle of depression and schizo-affective disorder. A path leading in a new direction, a turning point.

In our society, we are so often told about mind over matter. We are told that doing, achieving, success, healing is up to us. We are told that if we think positive, make the right choices, discipline ourselves and apply our minds to the task we will succeed. We are told we can do anything if we really want to.

In my case, my mind didn't work too well, to say the least. So, this advice was wrong. Its effect was to make me feel like even more of a failure.

Because schizo-affective disorder certainly felt like a ginormous failure on my part.

Failure to think, to function, to communicate, to act, to laugh.

It is also perceived that way by some in our society, that's when we get the "pull yourself together"! So, we get the thumbs down from within and from without, putting an incredible downward pressure on the spirit.

However, my family, friends, and doctors (I felt!) didn't see me that way.

To come back to my mind, in my case, I had to start the process of healing, any process of living, from the opposite side: matter first, mind to join in. In this instance it meant effort translated into action, translated into feeling better, translated into the capacity to do better, to think more clearly, physically, mentally, emotionally, tiny step by tiny step.

And it worked!

It made my doing (in this instance exercising) a reality: a change had taken place; I am not utterly powerless!

That's when I realised everything, every reality, every action, has two sides, each side the opposite of the other: physical/Spiritual, concrete/abstract, mind/matter, right/wrong, right/left, light/dark   light/heavy, black/white etc. etc....ad infinitum. And it can go either way: From one side to the other and vice versa and, there is a third component which determines, in part, which direction things can go: the self, through the choices we make.

But, at the same time, I had done it all before, yet I suffered terrible relapses.

So, what to do?

I had been trying so very hard to be really well, but I wasn't, not quite. I was functioning well, but I still felt pretty tense most of the time.

I kept searching.

2. MEDITATION

One thing that I hadn't tried, but had heard and read about, is the benefit of meditation. I am a   Radio National listener and an avid reader. I listened to programmes on meditation and on religion and on depression and on spirit, all the things I am interested in. I learnt that the Buddhists are the experts on meditation, and Buddhism is a lot about the mind. So, I wanted to make a start, to explore meditation.   By then, making a start was not impossibly hard anymore; I had a lot of practice.

One "thing" stopped me though. Meditation is quite trendy these days and is often portrayed as this mysterious and difficult thing to do. For example, one had to empty one's mind of one's thoughts and be able to be calm and completely still for a period of time in order to do it "properly". We need a "guru" to teach us. This guru will tell us how and what to do and, of course, we will pay him or her handsomely for it, not only in money but in reverence also.

Well, I was not calm inside, my mind was still agitated. _**I've been told all my life what I could NOT do**_ – at school and in religious education especially – so I was not going to put myself under the authority of anyone else if I could help it. At the same time, I didn't know anything about meditation, so I needed someone to teach me.

Where to go for the "right" help?

I decided I'd visit the big Buddhist Temple in Wollongong. I had seen it being built when driving past and, if nothing else, it looks beautiful. Shaune, Mariya, Serge and Margot came as well. It was an interesting visit, an encounter with a different way of thinking. On the way out, Margot gave us a book she had bought in the shop as a thank you for the lift. This book was: "Being Peace" by Thich Nhat Hanh. I read it and it resonated with me.

In it, it says: **"suffering is not enough".** This hit me in the face.

I didn't want to be sad, unhappy, and miserable. I had been fighting these feelings with all I've got and was still fighting them whenever they manifested. But as I continued reading, I realised it's not about denying the suffering – the negative – in my life, in me. It is about seeing the wonders as well in all of existence including in myself. As I read more and more of Thich Nhat Hanh, I also realised it is not about fighting, even those negative feelings, it is about making peace with them and therefore with myself because I am my thoughts, feelings, perceptions, body, and deeds.

So following Hanh's teachings I started meditation. And with meditation, as it was and is with exercising, I had to start from where I was at the time and take it from there. The first step was to learn to follow my breathing. Ten times: in…..out…..It was enough at the beginning, trying to put all my attention on the breath. Saying the action in my mind as I was doing it, resulting in: 1. action, 2. body (I was breathing with my body) and 3. Mind: being attentive to the breathing, working and being together in the present moment.

Every time my mind went wandering (and it did a lot of that) I brought my attention back to the breathing trying to reach 10 without interruption. It took a lot of practice, a lot of training because that is what it was: training in concentrating and building on it, like exercising. And, like everything worthwhile, it also took and still takes, time, effort, and persistence.

A "side effect "of this training is that while I was concentrating on my breathing I wasn't thinking and feeling that I should be doing something else, that I should hurry, that I was too busy, no time for breathing (ironic!), no time to stop; worrying that I am not doing enough, not achieving enough, feeling, and believing that I am not good enough. All these habitual thoughts going round and round in my head a lot of the time.

I know now that this is **extreme stress**: perceptions of lack of time and doubts about being good enough, feeling I am a fraud and being afraid that I am simply not good enough. I believed that I am not intelligent enough, but I know now that this low self-esteem, low or absent self-worth i.e., **Shame**, low or absent self-love, are the primary causes and simultaneously the primary results of my mental illness. Stress and shame are killers: literally and metaphorically. Stress and shame will attack wherever we have a vulnerability, it will worsen any difficulty or problem we might have, physical, mental, and emotional.

Too much stress is a major trigger of ill-being for everyone, but for me in particular, because I seem to feel every emotion extremely strongly (hypersensitivity) and also because, when I am stressed, I cannot slow down, let alone, escape my thinking. It is as though my mind does what she wants regardless of what I want!!!!

I suppose that's what the subconscious in action is.

Through meditation, I moved on to observing my feelings, thoughts, behaviours, body, and perceptions. I noticed that my mind was always rushing and that I did everything in a hurried manner.

I instituted what I call my Go-Slow Policy. Try to slow down everything I do. **No more rushing.**

Say NO to working too fast, playing too fast, thinking too fast. – However, it doesn't mean going to the other extreme and going too slowly. - Neither extreme is good: find the right equilibrium or balance for me between the two.

Say YES to what I am doing moment by moment with my attention on the doing (I do that by observing my movements and saying the action in my mind while doing it). The effect of this little exercise is that I am present in the here and now.

And something astonishing happened! Slowing down didn't limit my capacity to do what was needed or what I wanted to do. It was the opposite! It enhanced those capacities! PARADOX!

This is because, in order to slow down, I had to focus on what I was doing at the time. My doing became more efficient (focussed) and, most importantly, I wasn't using so much energy, so I wasn't feeling so fatigued, and I had energy left to do more!

I also had to make an effort to keep my mind on the task at hand. An effort of the mind to think about what I am actually doing now as opposed to being under the dictates of anger, frustration, fear, and helplessness. In these moments it was I, the observer above my wild mind, who controlled the thinking. *I controlled it from my consciousness not the other way around.* I didn't know that then, but I felt the effect of that exercise and it felt good. It is as though it allowed me to gather myself, it is as though I was lost, and it allowed me to come back to myself and to the present moment. The result, which I couldn't have envisaged, was a subtle awakening of my consciousness: **FINDING MYSELF**.

That's when I realised every action can go either way: helpful/unhelpful, good/bad, positive/negative, creative/destructive, right/left. And the opposite: unhelpful/helpful, bad/good, etc....

And that sometimes less can also be more and vice- versa PARADOX!

Every action is a balancing act between the two extremes: from nothing to all and vice- versa and the two opposite sides i.e., the contradiction, the paradox.

Getting the balance right i.e., **finding the point of equilibrium** is the key to "right" action. The point in time and at which the action has the most likelihood of succeeding. The point where I can be and do my best, the point of awareness and understanding the paradox (seeing both sides of the story and my role in it) and, with this information, being able to choose which way I'll go.

I did and still do this almost every day: training my mind to concentrate, to focus, training in slowing down because I can't do it fast and hard, it doesn't work. Training to take MY time (the right time for me: not too fast, not too slow). And in this process learning to set my own pace and allowing gentleness. And, there again, an extraordinary thing happened: doing things gently takes away the harshness present in everything, in every action and in me. And here again our society tells us: work hard, play hard, try harder. Wrong again, for me it is the opposite.

I have a tendency to try too hard and to take things too seriously. Fast and hard is no fun; on the contrary it is stressful, therefore counterproductive. In my case, it led to illness and dysfunction, and no one is the better for it, from society (treatment is costly) to my workplace (I couldn't work for quite some time) to my family (costly for us too, starting with joy and ease and, of course, money too**). Fast and hard excludes**

love because **it takes time** to be attentive to self and others and to be present.

The right time is also needed in order to enjoy each other's presence and what it is we are doing in the moment i.e., living this point in time! The same is true when alone: time to stop the relentless activities; patience and stillness are necessary to be in touch with our own consciousness. It simply can't be otherwise. By that I mean it is impossible to be connected with our consciousness while doing and thinking a thousand other things, we just end up dispersed, over excited, and very stressed. This makes it impossible to be centred or collected (together as one: body, perceptions, thoughts, feelings, deeds, and consciousness and in connection with our environment.)

That's when I realised, we, human beings also hold within ourselves the two opposites, the two extremes, including me and everyone else for that matter. We hold within ourselves the potential for good and the potential for bad; so, we can act towards good (helpfully, doing right , healthily) or towards bad (unhelpfully, doing wrong, unhealthily).Knowing what is good and what is not, is the key. Too much dispersion is unhelpful to this end and definitely so is too much stress !

It is also at around that time (I am talking about a time frame of several years here) that I came across the sentence:

Too much is the same as not enough.

So, how to know what is the helpful, the "right "manner or way for me to do or think something?? The way that leads to wellbeing?

Here again, to get to know a better way, I had to start from the beginning and my story can only start with me: myself: who I am and, start from where I was at the time. I sort of knew the story so far, but now I was not so sure about anything anymore. But I felt that there was more of me, deep inside, buried under that river of mud, the river of my thoughts.

So, start digging!   Trying to uncover the "real" me.

But hold your horses, Beatrice! Isn't this a bit self-indulgent? It is navel gazing, is it not? Who am I to think that spending time just thinking about myself is helpful? Surely it is egoistic and will lead to self-absorption rather than discovery?

However, I was already in the habit of meditating for a while almost every day. I did that even when my husband and children were around. They smiled and probably thought I was a bit "mad". Nonetheless, they tiptoed around me, and I continued on and we all noticed that it made me feel good, more settled and we all benefited because, in a family, when one is ill everyone suffers; when one is feeling good, everyone benefits.

Meditation is not only about breathing; it is also about observing myself, others, my environment, the world, and getting to know what's going on. And then working on acting and interacting, wanting peace and love for myself, those around me and possibly even extending further to my environment, the world and while I am at it : the universe! A tall order! (My children were not wrong!)

3. OBSERVING MYSELF

But, first, let's come back down to earth because I can only start from where I am.

"Know thyself", I read in a book on philosophy. It is long-established wisdom going back more than two thousand years. So, I figure, if it's good for the Greek philosophers and it has stood the test of time, it's good for me too. I therefore take it on board.

"To all our relationships we bring our own self" Stephanie Dowrick writes in her book: Intimacy & Solitude; I would add to all our perceptions and expressions **(the way we establish relationships) we bring our beliefs, our assumptions and our prejudices and <u>so do others.</u>**

When my first doctor and I parted, after the psychotherapy, he said to me "we have done a lot of work" and I thought "yeah definitely work for him and well paid too" but for me? However, I had tried to answer his probing as well as I could, as honestly as I could and for that I had to search deep down into myself. He expected me to answer his questions, so I had to somehow express myself, say something! And to be able to do that I had to work very hard indeed. So, **I realised it was work from my side too!**

I gave myself permission to continue the "psychotherapy" through introspection!

Still following Thich Nhat Hanh's teachings I wished to try to learn to better observe my feelings, my behaviour, and my thoughts and then, try to figure it out and make changes where needed.

But, in order to do that I needed to find out who I am and where I stood.

So, I needed to start at the origin of my illness: me.

4. ME

Me: the human being made out of flesh and bones

And also of fear, anger, sadness, bitterness

And also of needs, desires, and dreams (heart's desires, aspirations)

And also of love, joy, and peace

A separate, unique, individual yet interconnected to all that is, therefore free to be myself and, at the same time, interdependent upon everything else. PARADOX!

In order to understand how all this works the fundamental element I needed was to be present in my body and in my mind.

So, I learnt mindfulness which is a method to bring the I (Beatrice, the person, the human being) to life as it is now**, get real!** I learnt more techniques and methods to keep building up mindfulness; basically, I kept training: physically (exercising); mentally (learning as much as I can from writings, radio and observations, keeping up my practice in concentration and gentleness); emotionally (also observing thoughts and feelings and perceptions); spiritually (listening to my emotional heart and following it, listening to and following "good advice" when it feels right).

I continue to read Thich Nhat Hanh, I have also started reading the Bible, the Koran, the Tao Te Ching, philosophy and more, and I take advice from these. I wanted to go to the primary sources of explanations of what and how life is and how it works and then look at it from my point of view, try to understand from my perspective. I am also interested in the sciences. The effect of this curiosity is that it is generating more observations and I am learning new things all the time and I believe that I am gaining some new insights into life. It has become quite fascinating! And I have become quite intrigued by the interplay of all things, including me and everyone else. And it feels surprisingly good; it feels as though I am playing some part in the story. It is bringing to me a new sense of belonging to the world and a feeling of joy!

Thich Nhat Hanh says that whatever we do has to be for the benefit of both ourselves and those around us and everything. So, I ask myself this question regularly: is it good and right for me only or is it good and right for me **and** the people around me? I make a point of reminding myself that the most important thing is to love and be loved, to take the time to do what needs to be done **first**, have the time to give my family and friends and social contacts the attention they deserve **first** and also to be receptive to their love, **first** as well! (Three firsts - three-way street!) When it comes down and up to true love, who is counting?! I tried, and keep trying, my best to do that.

In order to be able to do my best I learnt that I have to include myself because we can't love others if we don't love ourselves. Therefore, it is ok to do things for my own benefit without feeling guilty that I am selfish and too self-absorbed, beliefs and feelings coming from my religious education, especially from the commandments: "Love the Lord your God with all your heart, with all your soul, with all your mind, and with all your strength. Thou shalt love thy neighbour as

yourself. There is no other commandment greater than these."
Mark 12: 29.

This was drummed into my head and, I guess, into every Catholic child's head. The trouble is my teachers dismissed the second half of this command: the bit about loving yourself!

Another teaching that is said in every Mass is "Lord, I am not worthy that you should enter under my roof, but only say the word and my soul shall be healed". I understood this as: I am not worthy, I am not good enough; and since I am excessively sensitive, it made a big impression on me. It was never explained to us that this statement came from a man who had authority among people and must have known his human worth and, at the same time, recognised the higher power of God, the divine power, and bowed to it freely.

But, as a child, I hadn't learnt my human worth and I was still dependant on adults for my wellbeing. Therefore, I didn't possess my own "authority" from which I could freely choose to surrender to the higher power of God. I realise now, as I am writing this book, that this "not being worthy" translated in my mind into *"I have no value"*.

5. THE CORE BELIEFS AND EMOTIONS THAT FORMED THIS TERRIBLE PAIN I WAS EXPERIENCING WHEN ILL

I became pretty good at observing my feelings. I could even be aware of them as they happened!

With the methods and training learnt through meditation, I could now turn my attention in a desired direction, reflect on a problem and try to figure it out; not all the time but enough of the time.

As soon as I was functioning well enough to write I had gotten into the habit of jotting down how I felt in an attempt to clear some of the confusion I experienced.

So, here it is:

Fear | Anger

Now, fear, this was the big one. It was so strong; I could taste it.

Fear is a force to be reckoned with.

Up until my illness, I didn't think of myself as fearful. Nobody does, and, in a lot of ways, I was, and I am courageous too. **PARADOX!**

But now that I am on the path of recovery, I do recognise it and I still feel it quite strongly at times.

I feel it in two ways:

1. *Social Anxiety*

What is anxiety? Anticipation of an imminent danger, spontaneous, automatic anticipated fear.

It seems it comes over me every time I have an interaction with anyone I perceive as having some kind of "authority" over me, in day-to-day occurrences: teachers, doctors, dealings with administration, or with anyone aggressive, especially if they are also impatient, or arrogant.

Or every time I feel I am being watched, simply people looking at me in an ordinary interaction,

this incredible tension rises in me: every nerve, muscle, tissue, cell, suddenly stands on high alert for no reason since, intellectually, I know very well that there is nothing to be so scared of.

I tell myself "This is really stupid! Get a grip" and I carry on "normally", and sometimes quite effectively I might add, at the expense of an immense effort of will; the only outward sign being a strong tremor in my hands, and eventually, when I am on my own, exhaustion.

Again, <u>at the depth of my illness</u>, I wasn't able to get a grip, I was so scared that I couldn't think at all, let alone carry on and I was in this heightened state most of the time resulting in me becoming completely paralysed. My brain stopped functioning and so did my emotional heart. My body too: lethargy set in.

As I got better and became conscious of this and started to understand the mechanics of it, I would imagine a situation which normally brings that reaction and replace my habitual reaction with a new, calmer response. I did this within meditation and slowly, with a huge amount of patience and practice, I could transfer this new response to real situations, changing something in the way I function. It didn't work all the time, but enough of the time to make a difference, to make it a little bit easier.

The medication also helps: it makes it less intense. However, although it helps with the symptoms, it doesn't address the cause of it, and I still experience those panic attacks from time to time.

This is something I've experienced for as long as I can remember, but I never knew what it was. I could definitely not recognise that it was fear at the root of the problem, and it is fear that has to be dealt with. It is the observation of the manner in which I act and of my feelings that allowed me to understand what was happening. I still had to discover why it is happening and more importantly how can I turn this chain of reactions around and stay calm?

The second way I feel anxiety is as this overwhelming, absolutely dreadful feeling of drowning, of sinking in a pool of viscous mud or of spiralling down the bottomless well.

I call it:

The vacuum effect and the black hole!

I only experience this when I am on my own.

It is as if my centre, my guts, my self (that inner sphere of personal courage, determination, and hope) has and is being sucked into nothingness and, once out there, I am outside of the world, looking in at it, looking at life, but I am excluded from it and no matter how much I want to come back**, I can't.**

Almost all communications, including Love, in and out, between myself and others and the world are severed: I am completely separate. I feel completely alone. It's not that I don't want to communicate I just can't, I don't know how. I've lost the capacity to do so. It's so bad that

I cannot feel that I exist.

I lose nearly all senses of perception and expression. I become frozen solid!

I feel sheer terror in my mind (the physical sensation of free fall into a well or drowning), in my body (strong chest pains, extreme tension, and nervousness) and I also feel an incomprehensible, bottomless sadness. That's when the idea of killing myself looks very sweet indeed. It is the only way I can see to escape the terror and sorrow; it seems to be the only possible way to find peace.

I call it: touching the void.

When I am in that state, I find being on my own unbearable. I absolutely need somebody else's presence to give me a little bit of reassurance and of life's energy, (warmth). It seems to me that, deep down, I know that without it I will not be able to resist these very strong impulses (the temptation) to kill myself.

I was in the dark as to why I should feel that way and even as to how I actually felt. All I knew was the fear, the distress, and the confusion of it. It is only recently, as I learn more and more about myself, others, and the universe, that I try to understand how it works for me and I study my notes and follow treatment, that I can attempt to make some sense out of this nonsense. (madness).

And it starts with knowing what's going on and for that I need to be able to describe it, which is where writing it down became a means to understanding. It also happens to take some of the terror off this awful experience but there is a long way to go.

And it is taking a long time; I have a lot of learning to do.

I didn't behave aggressively when I was not in charge of myself (psychotic). I don't like violence.

So, I didn't think of anger as a big problem for me; however, I was wrong! I realise now that an immense frustration filled my heart, but I didn't act on it.

Joy Hope Love

Joy is totally absent when one is mentally ill; it is replaced by total discouragement and an immense sadness. A total disheartening of the mind, including of the emotional heart, and of the body as well; fatigue is a constant companion.

Joy is a fundamental element to well-being so if I am going to go towards good health, joy must be included in the equation.

How?   Positive thinking?

Positive thinking is a lie and pretending that I am happy or forcing a belief in an outside God's intervention doesn't work for me because I know that it is not the truth at this time, it is not my reality, and I cannot afford to try to convince myself of something that is not real! I am confused enough as it is!

When I am told or taught or I tell myself something is the truth and I sense something else is, it creates an incoherence in my mind, and it definitely doesn't feel right. When what I am being told matches my perception and my experience, when my thinking fits in with my experience, then it feels right and that's a very good feeling even if I am dealing with difficulties. It gives me some guidance as to what to do next and it's quite simple: do more of the things that feel right; avoid or change the things that don't. The same applies to what I am being told: from publicity to religion, to opinions, to societal beliefs, to health advice and so on. If it doesn't feel right, I don't take it as the correct way for me to think, to believe and/or to act even when I differ from the majority or the status quo.

At the same time, I found (from my readings of Thich Nhat Hanh) that joy is also a practice not just a gift from on high. I believe it is actually both and I started to understand that in order to be able to touch joy, to feel joy, I have to reach out. I needed to find a path leading up to joy or, in other words, I needed to develop the capacity to create and experience joy; not however, as excitement, but as simply being able to enjoy and appreciate the day-to-day living.

But how do I start the momentum to go uphill? I needed to find a way to tweak perceptions, thoughts, feelings, interactions out of the misery cycle.

The support I received from family and friends made me realise with a new intensity how precious their presence in my life is. In turn, that realisation filled me with gratitude. Gratitude is a bringer of love and joy, and it furthered my motivation to be a good wife, mother, friend etc. generating more love and joy. I never take it for granted now. The love between us had always been there but I had lost the perception and the capacity for it for a while, and now that I could feel it again, I remind myself regularly how precious everyone is and how much we need each other, and I savour every contact I have with them. This doesn't mean that it is perfect bliss all the time, which would definitely be neither realistic nor the truth.

The key elements in being able to perceive emotions again are time and presence: being right here right now with my attention on myself and the other and on the doing (as opposed to on myself only, or on the other only, or far away in the past, or in the future or in dreamland or in "fearland").

All this takes time, consciousness (attention) and the effort to give and receive love; we can't do it any other way. Being loved and loving brings a lot of joy.

So, here I find myself again: the path it seems is my go-slow policy (take the time that's needed, NO RUSH!) concentration, mindfulness and body training and the desire and the deeds to think and act in good faith; wanting peace, love and joy for myself and others and all. I do need a lot of training and practice in order to be able to develop these skills, no doubts about that!

Another way of triggering joy is through positive experiences. **<u>We</u> (and I very much so) <u>all absolutely</u> need <u>to do something constructive</u>** to feel that we are alive, to feel that we exist, that we belong, and to nourish our spirit. We usually fulfil this need through our work, that's why people who cannot work get so dispirited and that is one more reason why exercise is so helpful. It was a way for me to start the ball rolling towards doing something positive. When I actually managed to do something, it gave me cause to be pleased with my effort and it made me realise that I can do something towards helping myself feeling a bit better. This positive feeling in turn reignited the **hope** that "things" can improve, can get better, that I can get better.

Hope, and the capacity to act on it, seems to lay the foundation (good ground) on which to build, and continue building on towards the improved capacity to function reasonably happily.

Joy, hope, love and the ability and the will to make an effort are an absolute necessity for living and being in good health. And when suffering my depression, they completely disappeared.

Positive experiences helped restore them into my life.

Things started really improving when I realised that I have to make a point of acknowledging my efforts to myself. For example, at the beginning, when people asked me what I was doing with myself and all I could say was "I am exercising for 10 minutes each day", to an outside person, it sounded pretty slack, it appeared as though I was not trying, so I was not going to get acknowledgement from others at that point. However, I knew what it took to do just that and I started to say to myself "well done, see you can do something "and, slowly, kept building on it.

Joy is also always available in the appreciation of beauty, music, art, nature, and science (including human nature), and in a job well done. Through gentle efforts and gentle actions and meditation I was relearning to be in touch with joy.

The primary motor here is effort. Effort is the activator that reignites the spark which turns on the light at the end of the tunnel.

It is an attempt to extend ourselves so as to reach out and fulfil our needs, aspirations, and desires.

We, and I included, often have the wrong idea about effort. We think that it must be strenuous, showy, even a bit glamorous to be valid. We think we must conquer our Everest, then we'll experience joy, then we'll be happy. This false idea puts joy out of reach, not within reach, and robs us of the hope and the realisation that "ordinary" life can be enjoyable and good, as well as sometimes sad and hard. **So-called ordinary or everyday life is real life! PARADOX!**

I remembered: too much is the same as not enough!

So, in effort, as it is with all things: too much is unhelpful and so too is not enough.

Again and again, it seems to me, the most helpful way is finding the right balance, the point of equilibrium, between not trying at all and trying too hard.

The point where not enough becomes enough and is not yet too much and vice versa!

And, before my illness, it was too hard that I was trying!

Trying too hard to be "good", being a bit of a perfectionist. This is a natural tendency I have, and it makes me take and do things much too seriously at times.

This constant call in our society to strive, to fight, and to compete in everything we do in order to get somewhere is misleading. It led me down the path of stress to misery not the path of joy to happiness. At the same time not trying at all leads to just as bad misery.

This constant call, in religion (any religion), to be "perfect" according to the hierarchy (which usually means to be subservient to them and the way they interpret the scripture) is also unhelpful, especially when it is at the expense of self-determination and self-love. Because the irony is we can't love others if we don't love ourselves. Love is about giving and receiving, it is an exchange, we can't give if we have nothing to give and that is the reality: it is how it is, it is not a choice. **It is an absolute necessity. It is the truth.**

And, belonging to this same truth, is the fact that we ALL deserve love and happiness, and we ALL have a right to self-determination. This is a gift from God at birth to every life form: the right, the duty, and the freedom (in human beings) to develop to our full potential.

Every human being needs to cultivate the qualities that will help him/her to reach this state. Some of those qualities are common to all: true Love, compassion, work, and equanimity (the belief, the knowledge, and the behaviour to match, that all men and women, including ourselves, are created equal and good.)

Some of those qualities are particular to each since we are unique. The best approach is to develop our natural tendencies and for that we need to know what these are (know thy - self)

Our deepest aspirations also tell us what we are meant to be, so to speak. My deepest aspiration has always been to be intelligent, that is what I wished for the most. Everyone is different so our aspirations vary too. There isn't a right or wrong, as long as these aspirations are not at the expense of someone else.

When we are denied access to the development of our potential through circumstances or wrongdoing or errors of judgement (all three in self and in others, internal and external) a strong yearning takes its place creating a vacuum.

A vacuum is a fundamental need not fulfilled. This vacuum sucks up a lot of our life's energy. The result in my case was I felt depleted and empty. This sense of emptiness was so strong in fact that it contributed to my feeling of not existing. <u>I couldn't feel any substance to my being, and that is the worst feeling ever.</u>

6. FEELING GOOD

Time went by. Life was pretty sweet now (as opposed to death previously). I felt bloody terrific.

So, now, finally, I can stop taking my medication I thought!

My doctor warned me of the risk of relapse, but I was confident I had it all figured out and that my continued exercise and meditation practices would stand me in good stead.

So, I did stop, very carefully, reducing it a little bit at a time, very slowly until I was free of medication.

Alleluia!

I was fine for three months, and then**: relapse!**

And with it, the sense of being alienated from this world as strong as ever....................

So, something more still had to change.

The evidence that I couldn't function and therefore be happy without medication became absolutely clear.

I had tried my very best to heal from schizo-affective disorder, but the illness was still here, in me. And that is an undeniable fact. It is a reality I couldn't change. No one (including myself) can ask of anyone to do more than one's best, it is simply impossible. It is our human condition that we all have our limits, our frailties, our faults. And one of mine is that my brain doesn't fire up properly due to a chemical imbalance, the consequences of which are that I can't think properly, I lose the ability to order my thinking if I don't take medication.

In my case

There was one thing I could do though: **give up** on my idea of being medication free, accept, surrender to how it is, and see that this is the way forward for me. Stop wanting to get rid of this beast, it is not going to go away!   Stop fighting, make peace with it and hopefully, while accepting the help offered to me, learn to master it! So that I decide, I choose how I live. It is not imposed on me by internal forces I do not know and therefore have no sovereignty over.

7. CHANGING ATTITUDES

I realised that I was wrong about the medication, for me it is not a choice but a necessity.

What had to change is not me and my illness, but my attitude towards it. This is because my illness is all mixed up with the healthy and good in me and by getting rid of the illness, I also get rid of a part of me. (Pema Chodron)

Pema Chodron says in her book: "The Wisdom of No Escape", that always thinking we must improve is a sort of subtle aggression against who we really are. The idea is not about trying to throw ourselves away and become something better. It's about befriending who we are already.

Help comes in many different forms. The medication is one of them. No matter how hard I try I simply can't function without it: that is how it is. So, I take it and I know now that I will need to take it for the rest of my life. (I have to write this down in case the idea that I don't need it springs in my mind again!) My mind has a habit of playing tricks on me but, by hook or by crook, I am going to outsmart it!

Does this mean that all I have to do is take the meds, be a good girl, do as I am told and all will be fine?

I wish it was that simple: but **THAT IS NOT HOW IT IS.**

I had taken meds over long periods during the last 10 years, and I still felt strong anxiety and the black hole effect at times, so there is definitely more to my well-being than chemicals.

I realised it is my attitude about myself and others and All that is the central axis of my experience of life.

It is self-esteem, ego, beliefs, perceptions, experiences (past and present), knowledge: as in what I have learnt and am still learning and take as the truth and the way I think that formed, and continues to form, this attitude. Because, like everything and everyone and all, it is not static, it moves and therefore changes. It is this movement that makes it possible for me and all to choose which direction I/we am/are going to go. Towards growth or regression?

Due to the fact that everything moves forwards (FLOWS), if we don't evolve or change, we fall behind and therefore regress.

So, it became clear to me that in order to be really healthy I need to understand the things that still cause pain in my body and mind. (The black hole, the void, anxiety, and the links with everything else.)

I need to reconfigure my thinking! I need a new system of thought!! Allow the audacious thought that maybe I can think clearly and see the interactions, the relationships between occurrences and people and I can take more right steps towards wellbeing.

It's about finding the "right" point of equilibrium in the interactions, knowing what's right and what's wrong and living accordingly. It's also about understanding the workings of relationships.

I am already on the path to this, a lot has unfolded since that first breakdown and I feel I have discovered much about myself, others, and the universe. It has been good for me and also for the people around me. I am now able to receive and to communicate much better and that includes my and others' love, respect, and gratitude. I've also discovered a new strength: I can say it when I disagree, even to people who are "above" me in the social scale. And when one is a mental health sufferer and, even more so in the case of a schizophrenic disorder, one is right down the bottom of that ladder. It's automatic. For example, I have been quite open about my attempts to write a book and I say it when I am asked what I do with myself. The automatic response is a question: what is the book about? So I tell the truth" it is about schizo-affective-disorder and it is my experience". I can feel the recoil from my interlocutor (only from people who don't really know me): Schizophrenia= losing it= craziness/chaos= violence. But sufferers are more than just the illness, we are fully human.

I disagree with violence; I believe violence is wrong and that belief stayed with me even when I lost my mind. This has been a great source of comfort to me.

So, I conclude that, so far, my new path had been good. I decided to continue on that path and see where it takes me.

3ᴿᴰ *PART*

AN INVESTIGATION INTO EVERYTHING!

Yes, I dare!

It's been ten years since the big crash.

Now I want to tie up the loose ends.

What still needs attention is:

1. Social anxiety

2. The black hole effect & void and

3. Panic attacks.

I've decided to try to go right down the bottom of it, look in front of it, behind it, underneath and above it. Look it right in the eyes. **However, not in a confronting way (wrestling with them) but instead in an understanding way.** (Contemplating the causes and conditions that brought on these issues and how to let go of them and form new responses that hopefully will lead to wellness).

Thich Nhat Hanh calls these (1/2/3/in my case) unwholesome mental formations and this is spot on.

What needs transforming is not me or others or the past or the world, that's not going to happen,

I can't – no one can. What I hope I can do though, is turn unwholesome thinking into wholesome thinking.

What I dare to hope to do is reorganise my thinking into a new peaceful system and order.

Social Anxiety, Panic, the Vacuum, and the Black hole revisited:

I have developed strategies to cope with these four and I am doing quite well. But now, in order to be as healthy as I can, in order to possibly free myself of those constraints, I need to deal with this irrational fear still present in my mind and body and therefore, still affecting my functioning.

This is because anxiety/fear ties me (or anyone who suffers this state), into a knot making it nearly impossible to control my reaction so I just contract tighter and tighter and, in turn, I seize up completely (freeze solid including my brain) making it nearly impossible to think and therefore to express myself. To others this appears as shyness or, as if I don't have anything interesting to say (not too smart), or, I am not interested in them (distance). When the peak of the anxiety has passed, I feel so ***stupid*** and ***ashamed*** for ***being so incapable***. Intellectually I know there is no reason to be intimidated and sometimes I over-compensate and become too forceful in the way I speak. Neither reaction is helpful for maintaining the best relationships.

And the good life, the healthy life is based on understanding relationships and being able to act on it i.e. make the connections. Everything is about relationships, that's how it is. The world is made of innumerable individual entities interacting with multiple others, or sometimes multiple entities relating with many others, all in an exquisite balance to produce the optimum outcome. (This last sentence comes from a add for Photonics). My experiences tell me that the optimum can be found at the point of equilibrium! The right balance.

When we ignore this fact and we don't see that we need to make an effort to take kind action to understand and participate in relationships, we either try too hard or not hard enough. We become awkward and tense and ill functioning and we think that we are not good enough; or the opposite: we think we are so good that we can't be wrong. Either way leads us to error: we feel inferior, lonely, and powerless - anger, discouragement and fear and even hatred arise within the self and are then projected towards others. Or the opposite occurs: arrogance/pride: we feel superior - disdain, contempt and even hatred arise in our heart, and they also get projected towards others. Both dynamics cause harm to self and others and beyond. Neither is right, in both cases we are kidding ourselves. In both cases, we are covering up for something else: fear! Fear of abandonment; fear of lack of approval; fear of not being someone. (Not being important i.e., being irrelevant.)

A good relationship is one where all the different elements and attributes interact in the right way creating equilibrium where life can flourish: one life – all life – the whole of life – as opposed to one at the expense of the other which causes an imbalance which in turn skews the equilibrium.

The lack of balance (too much or not enough in anything and everything, the extremes) contorts, contracts, twists, and hardens the heart strings and ties the nerves into knots, forming a tight ball towards which everything else gravitates! (I couldn't see or think outside of my misery when terribly depressed) and, as long as we don't see it and therefore don't deal with this imbalance, the cycle keeps perpetuating itself, driving the pull down, thus forming the vacuum. This, in turn, creates the black hole, creating these terrible feelings of emptiness: The Void!

As long as there is too much fear in me, especially in my heart, relationships (in my case only with people "in authority" and people I think are "superior" to me) cannot be rightfully equitable.

Fear also forces me into a defensive position because I just don't feel safe deep down inside me.

Being on the defensive means I unconsciously build walls around me to protect myself from getting hurt, but this has another effect and that is, I isolate myself. These walls form a prison. From there it doesn't take long to feel separate.

This sense of not being safe must come from experiences:

My father died when I and my twin were two years old, my other sister four and my brother six. My mother often talked of how he cared for us. His disappearance from our lives could not have been understood by us at that age and, to us, it must have been "abandonment". My mother found herself a widow with four kids under six; it must have been a very difficult time for her; a sad time, a frightful time, a lonely time. And there were the conflicts and the put downs from the in-laws.   My mother told me more than once how, as a very young child, I said to my paternal grandmother "I don't like you because you make my mum cry ". I believe I sensed these toxic emotions, and I absorbed them. They became mine.

As well as that I remember very clearly an instance of me, and my twin sister having been accused (mistakenly) of some pretty bad behaviour by a teacher at our school and my mother getting more and more furious as we tried desperately to tell her we hadn't done this. She didn't listen to us, she was so angry; she kept saying we were answering back. She didn't believe us, and she punished us severely. If my own mother, the only person who really cared about us, could treat us like this and hurt us so much then there was nowhere safe, and I was powerless to stop getting hurt.

I understand now that my mother was wrong in this instance. I also understand that she herself was raised to believe the "authorities". And I know that we all get it wrong sometimes. I also knew then and now that she loved me and my siblings more than anything; that fact I have never doubted.

This love also became mine. This is what allowed me, in turn, to love my husband and children.

Then there was the abuse I suffered as a child. I sense things very strongly and sexual and power abuse (it is both) is not only a physical experience. It is a mental, emotional and a spiritual experience as well. That is because it involves the act of being touched; my own body, which should belong to me only, being used. These touches felt awful. As well, there were the toxic emotions of lust and disregard of me being a person, directed at me and, somehow, they permeated my mind, my heart, and my guts.

To the perpetrator, at that time, you are only **an object** to be used to satisfy his sick desires and you can sense it even though you don't know what is happening. I believe every child victim of abuse can feel what I would now call **non-being** (not being treated as a fellow human being, not mattering at all, being demeaned, and being treated as insubstantial…) and that stays with us in our memory and gets stored in our subconscious.

And then, there are our own emotions: we feel absolutely awful, it can't be right! But we don't understand what is happening and there is nothing we can do to stop it. All this results in terrible pain, terror, confusion, utter powerlessness and fear which in turn we identify with, and these feelings become part of who we are (our personality/our identity). Further along, as we develop, these feelings too develop to form a body of depreciating beliefs: the "dementor" inside, a tight ball of pain which, in turn, attracts more pain through our selves being constantly on the defensive and **through having been robbed of the sense of confidence that life is good and so are we. A sense of insecurity and fear takes its place.** This, in turn, adds even more strength to the vacuum and the black hole.

As a child, like all children, I was still at the beginning of learning about life. These experiences taught me that things are **definitely not OK** and, apart from my twin, there is no one I can fully trust.

These beliefs, in turn, shaped my perception of the world; when you believe that things are not ok that is what you see! It led to the development of wrong (as in erroneous) ideas about myself (thinking I am inferior, thinking I don't matter, thinking I am not intelligent enough) and "wrong" ideas about others too (fearing them, thinking they are better than me, more knowing than me, superior to me.) And the wrong idea about the world, seeing the negative only, not seeing the wonders anymore.

At the same time, I was trying to do my best and I also had "some" sense that I was ok! PARADOX!

These denigrating feelings and the confusion make it very hard to understand the workings of interactions/relationships in life, in turn making it very difficult for me, (and every other sufferer of child sexual abuse, I am sure), to find our way in life and to learn how to progress. This is because in learning, as it is in everything, to comprehend and absorb new information, we need a solid and clear base on which to connect the new information. We need some confidence that we are capable, and deserving, to build on it; we need *to know and trust* that we have the intelligence and the entitlement to do well. We need a healthy sense of worth, *self-esteem and ego:* neither too much nor not enough.

We need to find the point of equilibrium within and without, in the interaction with other people and in the world, and beyond.

1. EQUANIMITY

So, these unwholesome mental formations made it just about impossible for me to develop to my full potential and, as long as these beliefs remain unchanged this will keep perpetuating itself.

That's how I felt deep down, I had that unexplainable sense that "something" was wrong, it sometimes felt as though I couldn't breathe freely; I often felt sort of tied down and therefore I was hindered in my ability to do the things I really wanted to. I often couldn't "get "what I was taught, and I also often couldn't quite believe what I was being told; I just couldn't match it with my experiences and with how I saw things i.e., my own perceptions. It didn't make sense to me; *it didn't feel true to me.* It's only lately that I have become conscious of the fact that *this gave rise to an immense frustration: a real lot of anger!*

But, I believed very strongly that anger is wrong; on the other hand, I did have this incredible anger in me. This reinforced my beliefs that I am somehow not good enough. The "dementor" loves anger, it feeds on it!   And becomes stronger!

I didn't want to be an angry "beast" so I didn't act on my anger; I realise now that I tried to ignore it and therefore repressed it. However, anger doesn't simply go away because you don't want it, it builds up inside (underground so to speak) generating this incredible tension and tightness I felt.

So, I, like all abuse sufferers, had to make my way through life with this fear, anger, tension, confusion, and **lack of trust** in me. The consequences of this is that every endeavour becomes much more difficult and, at times of stress, even too hard, triggering illness and putting the realisation of my deepest aspirations, my full potential, even further out of reach, leaving me wanting!

Because something is missing! And it manifests in the form of a strong yearning for the recognition that I am here, I belong in this world, and I am good enough.

And what was it that was missing? MATTERING i.e., substantiality, a sense that my life matters, that my story matters and CONFIDENCE i.e., Trust in Self, the natural belief and knowledge that I am fundamentally good and that I do have what it takes to cope in times of difficulties with resilience and courage and that most others are like this too. And, I have now discovered as I am writing this book: **Trust in God!**

God as the source of love and goodness, real, present and "working" through the kindness and love shown to me by others and, also, through my own efforts.

AND God as the creator of the "system "of nature i.e. The Higher Order because the arrangement in nature is not haphazard, life follows an order and we, human beings, are subjected to IT as we are part of nature. That's the reality as I see it now.

However, I have also learnt that I need to acknowledge that evil is real too and one can be touched by it through the evil deeds of abusers (sexual and, also, economic, political, physical, verbal, etc.) and through our own wrong doings; that is if we have done wrong! Contrary to some still widespread teachings, good people don't go around sinning all the time. As long as we do the best we can, it is good even if we get it wrong sometimes, even if we are weak sometimes. After all we are only humans! So, I do not accept this way of thinking anymore, it leads to exclusion (you are just a sinner, how could you possibly pretend to goodness) and feelings of guilt, shame, and smallness. In my experience, most people around me try to do what's right and so do I and that is enough. God doesn't ask the impossible and, anyway, the more I think about it the more I see perfection as an attribute of evil, not as an attribute of goodness.

However, I have been touched by evil through the abuse and the frequent negative and unhelpful criticisms (put downs) I've received, and the aftereffects of these injuries are still being felt.

This, I now feel, demands a response in order to reclaim my "own ground", the trust that I, as well as others, am good enough, the belief that I am neither inferior nor superior to others and vice versa and the sense that I do belong to this world, I am not separate (different). It demands a response so that I can develop and acquire the quality of equanimity which has a vital role in redressing the balance, in finding equilibrium in my existence: **the right balance.**

God's exquisite balance! And therefore be (in my small way) in harmony with God's Order!

Starting with my mind, it's a tall order indeed!

As long as we don't address these fundamental issues, I, and all who suffer a lack of substantiality (a sense of non-being), will approach everything in life from a very weak place, a place of inferiority and fear. In other words, abuse makes us meek, and we are afraid to take our rightful place in the story of life. In consequence we will remain disempowered, unwell, and very vulnerable to further hurts.

I used to have this strong sense that I had been forgotten, ignored, by society and by God, resulting in my feelings of alienation.

2. SPIRITUAL SUBSTANCE: FAITH AND MEANING

And yet, I was very lucky! I also experienced lots of Love and care and I received a very strong appreciation of the beauty of life. (In my nature and from my mum). Nature and nurture: both and both ways, not one versus the other.

And the consequences of this are that I also had the capacity, at times, to enjoy life, to love and to care and the capacity to say "No" to aggression. All the support I received when I was completely down restored my **faith** in human beings and, surprisingly, in myself too! The continuity of people's love and kindness through a time in which I was not able to reciprocate, was the beginning of a new realisation (new in the way I perceived it, I have become much more aware), **I now know in my heart and in my thinking** that I, and they, **do matter**, in fact our lives matter very much, in other words: we **mean** a lot to each other and we can feel the effects of this.

It is how we connect with one another and All that bring purpose and meaning to our lives.

Isn't it ironic, it took me to be completely empty to discover new meaning. It took me to be completely lost to find a new way. I didn't know what was real and what was an illusion. Through my search for developing the capacity to distinguish the two: separate the wheat from the weeds, acquire the knowledge of what's right (helpful, real) and what's wrong (unhelpful, false, illusion) the heavy fog in which I had lost myself has lifted and a new order has come in where I previously had confusion and dissonance only.

And that's when I realised that in the heart of every and all reality (i.e., what is!) And how it works: the truth! (I.e. how it is!) there is a contradiction. The truth can only be so when complete and comprises the two opposites. Half-truths are misunderstandings and therefore, lead to errors of judgement and errors of action, mistakes (we do the wrong thing, quite often unknowingly.) **We can be wrong about what's right!** (Plato and Socrates said it too!)

I can also see now the reality of interconnectedness. There is no way that I could have recovered (gotten out of the black hole) on my own. I was lost in darkness and people around me came to my aid and with their kindness they also brought some light to me. As time went on, I could feel their care and I felt the better for it (a subtle uplifting of my spirit and the co-arising of trust). With that light I was able to slowly find my way to wellbeing.

3. UNDERSTANDING

Understanding what's going on is the key to being able to take the right action towards wellness.

And, what I understand now, is that in order to liberate myself from the grip of the "dementor", I have to play my part in the battle. I must speak out! I must send this poison to where it belongs: into oblivion. I know that as long as I keep these toxic feelings in me, they will keep being active no matter what else I do, so I need to take action to neutralise them. The most fundamental action is to go about healing my sense of being, in order to develop the capacity to let go and release it, get it out of, my mind and body. I still think "bastard" when Didi comes into my mind, I still feel "off" if I am touched on my breasts.

And this battle is of good AND evil, i.e., right, and wrong. The truth is in the "and", since there is a contradiction within every reality: it comprises both opposites: PARADOX!

And it goes both ways.

And the most fundamental "battle" is between being human and non-being.

Thich Nhat Hanh (my adopted teacher) says that the fear of abandonment is universal.

I understand that, in our western society, the fear of being left to die is negligible; however, the fear of non-being (i.e. not being someone, not mattering to anyone, alienation and loneliness) is very much alive! PARADOX!

We all search for meaning (feeling and knowing that we matter, that our life is relevant, and that we are important) .... I am not alone!   <u>I am "normal"!</u>

Hugh Mackay says in his book "Right & Wrong": "The more I listen to people talking about their lives, and the more I ponder the highs and lows of human behaviour, the more I'm convinced that, in a society like ours, the most fundamental of all human needs is the need to be taken seriously.

Everything else flows from that."

Since reality is made of pairs of opposites, I also understand that there is light and darkness in everything and everyone. The deepest darkness is what I call the black hole, the void or emptiness: a lack of the realisation of the self mattering, which is caused by the concepts and ideas I developed from my experiences, information, and teachings I was given as a child (conditioning). And continuing through adulthood through my own and others mistaken beliefs and wrong information, from incomplete to bias to plainly false: very unhelpful.

But, also, I believe now, that a bit of empty space in my soul is good: there is room for something new to come in, for example new ideas of truth (i.e., what's real: very helpful). **PARADOX!**

So, the first step is seeing the reality, the truth, how it is and how it works! Then comes understanding what is right (helpful) and what is wrong (unhelpful). This means accepting what is, and from this platform developing and practising discernment and taking the next step based on the present situation, and on the willingness to be of benefit to myself and also to others. This the key to wellbeing.

Being able to choose the light i.e., making the right judgement and decisions on how I conduct my life and acting on these is the way to go forwards, but I can't do this alone: I absolutely need the love, kindness, and knowledge of others. We all do need each other! It is simply impossible to exist and live by ourselves or for ourselves only (we become a lost soul or a tyrant, both ways lead to goodness being extinguished and life will also be extinguished.)

So, my being fiercely independent was an illusion and I now surrender to the reality of interbeing (everything and everyone being related to everything else) and I can see that every one of us, in order to be healthy and well in body, mind and in action needs guidance from our conscience and, also, from outside of ourselves. Because, whether we realise it or not, we are not separate and also because, alone, we just can't know what to think and what action to take and how to go about it sometimes. (Even all together we don't know everything, the mystery remains!)

So, I decided to adopt Jesus as my teacher too!

What I wish to learn is more about equanimity. This is because there is still a semi- regular experience in my life that troubles me a great deal. The situation is this: I am in a social conversation, it can be in a group setting, a gathering, or a one-to-one setting, it doesn't matter.

What does matter to me though is that in the interchange of ideas and chit-chat about what we are up to - what's happening in our lives, I often get a feeling of going down i.e. I deflate, I feel myself getting smaller and smaller **and it hurts.**

This happens when someone boasts about their "fantastic" activities or their "oh so important busyness," everyone (who is someone of course!) is so busy these days! Or they might say: "I don't have the time for this, I work!" (as opposed to me; I have now retired from paid work) or, they carry on about the great things about something or someone else "so and so is so amazing, so bright, etc. etc."

The dynamic, as I understand it now, is: when a person raises their own status or the status of a third party with me, a sufferer of **a lack of confidence, self-esteem and ego**, (a healthy sense of individuality - self, neither too much - nor not enough) it automatically pushes me down because it hits right there in the middle of the wound in my soul. The wound created by the black hole, the void, and my inferiority complex. My mind thinks: so, and so is so wonderful and I am not. The balance of esteem is pulled right up on one side, but not my side and is therefore pushed right down on the other side, my side.

The inference, **in my perception and caused by my beliefs and premises, (the pre-existing "Dementor" inside)** is that I am not as good as the person I am talking to, or the person talked about, and I am not on the same level; therefore, it reinforces these notions of inferiority and of not being good enough and I feel their effects. When faced with boasting, my reaction was to retreat and not respond because it felt unsettling, and I didn't know why, and I didn't know what to say. And it would feel like I'd been somehow treated as meaning less than others again and this resulted in my being less capable of expressing my side of the story and therefore participating freely and easily in the discussion. In turn," the other side" perceives me as somehow lesser (because of the combination of my demeanour and their own "idealisation" of self and others). The consequences are that a kind of deep **sadness** and **emptiness** filled my heart again and again.

In one specific occurrence of this phenomenon, I confided to two very close friends of mine who were with me at the time. They too detected a bit of self-gratification on the part of the "boaster", but their reaction was quite different from mine; they certainly didn't feel any pushdown on their sense of being! They just shrugged it off as being part and parcel of socialising. And that's the way it should be! A bit of self-gratification is normal, it happens quite often, and we all do it when we are pleased with ourselves, there is no harm meant by it. (As opposed to arrogance which is very harmful).

However, the fact is, it does hurt me and makes me feel smaller. The hurt raises feelings of dislike (aversion) towards the person or people involved, feelings of enmity in my heart. In turn, the "other" senses this aversion towards him/her and reacts to it with their own aversion towards me and more enmity is thus created and so on back and forth. And so, the negative spiral is put into motion and takes off. This happens in the depths of being; of course at the intellectual level (on the surface) we don't realise what is really happening and we stay civilised, but true communication is not possible under these circumstances.

This dynamic separates me from the "other "; I feel as though I'm in a different (lower) dimension, alone. Too much of this happening can crush anyone. And when I was so low (depressed) I saw everyone as higher than me and since, at that time, I wasn't able to do anything, seeing and hearing about what others could do triggered this dynamic time and time again, and though I didn't understand I felt separate and a deep sadness at my inability to participate wholesomely in conversations, my inability to play my part in the dialogue, my inability to work, my inability to belong, **my inability to participate in life.**

I wished to find an answer to these sinking, diminishing and negative feelings and to the enmity that follows. And, hopefully, develop the ability to respond in a much more positive way for myself and for the other (a win-win situation).

How?   That was my question.

4. METTA BEHAVANA AND PRAYER

Soon after I started reading Thich Nhat Hanh, I attended an introduction to meditation course in a Buddhist centre. There I learnt about a different kind of meditation called Metta Behavana. Metta in Buddhism is loving-kindness (what I call true love, gentle love, the love Jesus talked about). The purpose of this meditation is the producing and sending of true love (metta) towards self (this immediately implies we are someone), towards someone neutral to us, towards someone we like and towards someone we don't like and towards all.

I practiced this "exercise" regularly and as honestly as I could. I continue to do so. At first, in the category of someone I didn't like, I chose people towards whom I just felt slight annoyance or dislike or people I felt uncomfortable with, social contacts I couldn't quite enjoy even though I wished to.

And the most extraordinary thing happened, my feelings towards them slowly changed, my perception of them changed. I started to see that they too have vulnerabilities; they too are trying to make themselves happy. With time I started to see that they too have emptiness inside themselves.

I started to see that *we* human beings all share in this emptiness. From this "hole" comes longing and longing tells us what we need according to our nature. It is the hunger of the soul.

And what we need most in our societies of abundance is true love, (and true love needs time i.e., patience to grow and practice) and social relevance (feeling that we matter, are being taken seriously) and that is what everyone is fundamentally battling for, just like me. And, like love, we get a fair share of our sense of relevance, our sense of meaning, through the way others reflect back to us.

But to be heard, we need to speak as well. To become relevant, we need to approach others and make contact. One cannot happen without the other, that's how it works! That's how God set it up: we need to be able to give as we need to be able to receive: that's the right equilibrium!

And to be able to make positive contact each of us needs presence in this moment in time and true love (loving-kindness), the desire and the will to act in a way that benefits both sides and vice versa.

As I try to understand and follow, I can see that not enough ego/low self-esteem is unhelpful therefore wrong (in error) and so is self-righteousness/ too much ego. I realised that this is how my point of being was not in equilibrium between me, others, and the world. I realise that this is my main obstacle on the way to well-being.

When not enough ego meets with too much ego, like a see-saw one goes down and the other comes up. This happens unconsciously most of the time. At the extremes, where it is a case of subjugation and tyranny, this is evil and luckily this is not my reality. It is my view and my experience that to acquire and develop the quality of equanimity, as in evenness and peace of mind, and to be able to sustain it, I have needed to heal the ego, and it is a continuous process.

A healthy ego, neither too much nor not enough; an ego in equilibrium: the right balance, that's the happy way.

Simultaneously, I discovered that all of us human beings have a strong tendency to perceive things as one way or the other and we form our opinions, ideas and decisions based on this error of judgement.

If it's not this way, it must be that other way or if it's black it can't be white! This is how our mind comprehends "things" and life, but it is mistaken since the facts are that the reality is both at the same time and goes both ways. **PARADOX!** So, the truth is: I and others can be doing well at the same time; someone else doing well doesn't necessarily mean I don't measure up! Life doesn't need to be a competition, true life is not only about calculation, it is my way of thinking that makes it so, and **it is not for real!**

As I read Genesis, I also came to realise that by the fact that I was born i.e., created in the spiritual realm as well as the physical, I am already someone, and it is good, therefore the pursuit of being relevant, to find meaning is back to front, **the truth is I am already relevant! And so it is for everyone else too! Life is sacred, all life, the whole of life. Real life is inclusive not exclusive.**

So, my being here is already meaningful, the "trick" is to really see it and feel it!

For that to happen I needed to recalibrate my assumptions, notions, and concepts. Observe, question and reason, basing this on what's real i.e., the facts and from there reform a new opinion.

I needed to develop a new philosophy of life, the understanding of how it is (reality and truth) and how it works: what is helpful, what is not and is it really so? I needed to question everything.

As I read how Jesus acted, I also noticed that he healed lots of people. He didn't judge them before doing so; he didn't choose who would be healed or not according to their "merits". In fact, it is the sufferer or their kin who approached Jesus and hoped to be healed, and he always healed them.

This tells me that I too have to stop judging myself and others: just let others be themselves and, for my part, be the best I can, in a light-hearted way since my natural tendency is to be too serious; allowing for a bit of silliness sometimes is part of the equilibrium.

If it's good enough for Jesus/God, it's good enough for me! It is time to accept who I am and tell these horrible, nagging feelings in my head and my heart to get lost. So, instead of constantly finding faults (shortcomings) in myself, I am starting to also recognise and value the good things that I have done and still make the effort to do, and I am enjoying the benefit without guilt. And that inner voice telling me to try harder and harder all the time and that whatever I do will never be good enough is becoming fainter and fainter as I grow stronger.

At the same time, when I can sense (and the trouble is, I sense emotions very strongly and I sense the push and pull of interactions) critical judgment coming to me from the person(s) I am relating to, I also know that he or she or they are also forming their own judgments. These are based on their perceptions, the information they received and are still receiving (and these days we are bombarded with information, a lot of which might have a hidden agenda behind it, like greed, power, self-gratification) and on their own self-beliefs, **especially on their own need to fill the void.**

So, I understand better that both, I and my interlocutor, have our frailties and that we all get it wrong sometimes and now it is compassion that arises in me instead of hurt, anger and enmity. This reconciles me with the other instead of separating us.

So, I and others have more in common than I had thought! I might even share some traits with people "In authority"!! God help us!!!!!

So, my sense of place is changing and with that my perspective as well. From my new point of view

life is very good and beautiful indeed as well as, sometimes, frightening, and ugly.

What is also very real and **can't be ignored** is malfeasance and malevolence; child abuse is of the worst kind because as a child we are unknowing and powerless to defend ourselves. The perpetrators also often present themselves as friendly and as "good citizens" and are seen as such by society.

<u>**The hypocrisy**</u> is huge and leads to great confusion in our minds.

It is only since I truly faced my fears and complexes that "things" started to shift back towards a more stable place. I now know that, when we are the victim of malfeasance, it demands an answer from us so that we can keep our inner strength and dignity. And, I am convinced, that in order to do this, as adults, the way to finding our equilibrium (a sense of equity of being and evenness of mind) comes through the addressing of these issues.

So first, recognise ownership of these terrible feelings, but not responsibility as we are always told.

Responsibility implies blame; I reject blame for me feeling so despondent when I was ill and I also understand that we, sufferers of mental illness, are not guilty of creating our illnesses either.

However, ownership and acceptance that this is the way it is at this time, this is the reality, and recognition that this way is producing lots of pain and misery for self and for people around us is paramount.

So, stop hiding! Stop running away from it all, stop being so busy, even so busy thinking! Wanting too hard to put things right, <u>do the opposite</u>: **slow down and look with great care into** the consequences of the abuses and the lack of trust and faith in self and in others and in the world, rather than striving to let go and forgive. Face it and work through it with the right help and with incredible patience, gentleness, and compassion.

Take and allow the necessary time, no forcing, neither trying too much nor not trying enough.

Re-establish justice of being, claim our rightful place in the story of life. Only then can we freely let go and possibly forgive. I, personally, let God decide on that last one.

5. TURN THE OTHER CHEEK

But Jesus said: "turn the other cheek" Matthew 5:38-39 Luke 6:29	so how does this fit in with my idea of facing malfeasance and claiming justice?

And it is not only my idea. We are all familiar with the quote of Edmund Burke: "All that is necessary for the triumph of evil is that good men do nothing."

And we know it is true.

I believe it is the same at the personal level. We need to respond to abuse and put downs and hypocrisy, as opposed to doing nothing and continuing to suffer the consequences.

In a book on Buddhist equanimity, I read that one of the practices towards developing it, is to fully experience (in my situation) the anger, the fear, the anxiety, the sorrow, and the confusion that "lurks at our core" (Ezra Bayda). Following these instructions, and in the context of meditation, I have now started to bring these feelings into my awareness, I breathe them right into the centre of the chest, slowly, with all the gentleness and care I can master, and then I simply let it be: It is what it is, it is how it is.

Stay with it; refrain from running away, from striking back, from going on the defensive, even from tightening up and closing down.

Just stay with it and **do nothing!** Refrain from judgements, evaluation, and especially fear! Just stay with the truth, how it really is and, at the same time, speak the truth. **Paradox!**

You wouldn't believe the courage it takes to "do" nothing and speak up!

That's one of the greatest paradoxes! Doing nothing in that situation is doing something very helpful. Staying with what is, means I stay present within the reality and my thoughts don't spin off uncontrollably; I just keep my attention on the breath and on how I feel right now, right here, what I sense. I don't try to evaluate anything. The instruction is to just gently keep my attention on the breathing and let it be. And, what happens (not every time, but enough of the time) is that, mysteriously, subtly, somehow, my experience of difficulty mutates into clarity and peace.

Peace in the sense that the compulsion to shy away, to be silent, to rush, the push to try harder and harder, to be more, to strive towards a goal, are mostly gone. Fear, anxiety, anger, stress are losing their "stronghold" on me and I can express myself.

A new state of mind has developed. **What liberation!**

I happen to believe that "turn the other cheek" means this dynamism. When we are confronted with aggression and hypocrisy (the "Dementors" inside and out) do not react with more of the same: fear, confusion, or/and aggression ourselves, but present and act from the other side: **the reverse way to automatic, instinctual," feral" reaction**, instead of retreating and trying to disappear in front of these "difficulties" (demons !) FACE them, with God's help and employing God's attributes, answer with truth, mercy, and love. However, this doesn't mean giving up our own ground. Jesus never retreated from His teachings, even in the face of death.

Evil (abusers, extremists) doesn't know truth, mercy, and love, so the "right" response might well be decisive action based on the truth - i.e., how it really is now, including an understanding of the paradox, so that the action is appropriate to the situation. At the same time, remember to keep these attributes in our hearts so that we don't, ourselves, fall into the trap of evil. So that we don't become "something like itself".

As well as we can, it's not going to be perfect and it's certainly not the easy way.

As long as we keep trying to ignore the reality and keep fleeing from it, we will not be able to change paths and therefore, possibly (it's not entirely up to us), find a new way towards well-being. If we don't speak up, evil will gnaw at our insides and make us sick.

My idea of well-being has evolved. Well-being to me now is Peace of Mind and one's rightful place in life, i.e. Present as a human being, as opposed to dispersed, fragmented, and completely lost in conditioned thinking mechanisms and in fear and sorrow. (This I have learnt from experiences, and it is also genetic.)

As long as we keep ignoring abuse and running away from it, we will not be empowered to act in a helpful way. We will stay in error, powerlessness and therefore FEAR and the abusers will keep abusing.

As I try to practice this teaching, extraordinarily, unexplainably, I feel myself growing stronger and so is my faith in myself, in others, in the world, in God.

The writing of this book is my way of responding to the abuse. I feel that I now also have my own "authority" (some knowledge and strength) from which I can choose how I live, including organising and guiding my thoughts. At the same time, I realise that there is a "Higher Power" than me.

PARADOX! I am both the boss of my life and not.

I surrender to that reality.

6. SO, WHAT NOW?

Who we think we are, seems to me to be the core of our emotional, spiritual, and physical well-being.

As I've learnt to get to know myself, I've discovered that I am a human being, present in my life, just like the other human beings. **I discovered that I belong.**

With my presence and helped by God, **I trust that I can know what's real and what's not, enough of the time** and I can see that the wonders in myself, in others and in the universe are real and so are the hurts, fear, anger, loss, errors (mistakes).

We all need to question our assumptions; it is easy to believe something that is not quite so. In his book: "Conversations with myself", Nelson Mandela says:

"But the process of illusion and disillusionment is part of life and goes on endlessly."

In mental illness our thinking and our beliefs are not based on the complete reality i.e., the truth.

The way we think plays a fundamental role in our power to determine how we conduct our lives and how we are.

For example, I thought I was not good enough and not intelligent; this led me towards timidity, withdrawal, sadness, and unhelpful defensiveness. Or, if we think and believe that if only, we were thinner or taller or we had a big house or travelled frequently or thousands of other things, all would be well. This way of thinking leads us to seek these superficial, material things, sometimes to the point of obsession and it is not well that we become, it is the opposite: stressed, unsatisfied and ill.

So, in my view, the process of questioning everything is vital to enable us to reset our minds based on real qualities, facts and values, thus allowing us to change the course of our thinking and our conduct towards a more helpful way. And, at the same time, it allows us to live peacefully and with a degree of ease without the need to constantly prove or validate our existence.

There are a lot of things we cannot change. Let it be. Paradox!

Conventional psychiatry in Australia doesn't offer anything to that effect. It offers medication, and it offers guidance (and I am very grateful for these) but, in severe cases, it also offers electroconvulsive therapy. Since I saw a program on TV

("Insight" on SBS) at the end of last year, I thank God every day for not having fallen into the hands of a proponent of electroconvulsive therapy. I am convinced that the outcome of my illness would have been very different indeed. Instead of being **enabled** I would have become disabled; it still sends shivers down my spine.

It took all the factors, understandings, and actions I describe in this book to get me to where I am now: peaceful and happy enough of the time, and able to share this peace and happiness with others. It has been and still is not necessarily easy, but it is deep contentment and gratitude that I now experience.

My experience and fear of non-being has evaporated,

replaced by Faith that my existence is worthwhile!

7. WHAT'S NEXT?

I don't know what will come next; no one knows what's around the corner. It's called uncertainty and it is a fact of life.

However, I continue on my new path of prayer, reflection, meditation, and learning. I also continue to exercise regularly (fundamental to well-being!) and eat and drink in moderation. I also remind myself regularly to slow down. When I feel some stress or compulsion coming on from outside or/and inside I tell myself, and therefore the stress, the pressure, and the compulsion too:

"NOT SO FAST!"   **There is nothing that can't wait. Let's not get carried away!**

I also accept that I am still, and always will be, vulnerable to upheavals in my mind, so I still go to my doctor every now and then for medication and advice.

My friends tell me that I am very disciplined. But they are wrong! Because it is not a discipline I impose on myself, it is a freedom I choose to exercise.

So, help me God. (If it's good enough for the President of the United States to ask for God's help, it's good enough for me!)

And help us all, we need it!

I now feel reasonably secure in my skin, my fear of others has been slowly diminishing and I hope to continue on that path. I am confident that I, together with those who love me (and vice versa), can deal with what life throws at us because I can feel the support and I can feel God's presence. And were harm to come our way, I trust that we would be strong enough to face it and take the "right" action, and/or accept it. And, hopefully, if God wills it, overcome it.

And I know that it doesn't mean that I and life will be all good all the time but enough of the time!

And there is one more "thing" that a "little" relapse just reminded me of: BB (my nickname) don't forget joy! This too can and needs to be nurtured as well as naturally received. BB: don't forget to relax and enjoy! Sometimes I can be so busy being good I forget about "fun", so being "bad" sometimes is being good! **PARADOX!**

So, life is not meant to be easy: right. But it's not meant to be that bloody difficult: too right.

As I look at it, I can see that, in the spiritual world, one plus one doesn't necessarily make two.

"And I think to myself" how extraordinary!

And I want to be in it, and I love it.

POST SCRIPTUM

Eight years have passed since I finished writing this book and I am continuing to learn. I have realised that the biggest obstacles to being well are SHAME (as in the belief that we are not good enough) and FEAR. Both are linked to fear of abandonment. If we are not good enough, how can we pretend to "connections and belonging" as Brené Brown says.

Abuse makes us meek; we are afraid we might get hurt again and we are afraid of reaching out. We build armour around ourselves for protection, we escape through addictions, or we shut down. The only remedy is participating in the work of love, including compassion for self, others, and All.

Ask God for guidance.

Take our cues from the teachings of people of conscience, past and present.

Learn to trust that there is indeed a Loving Higher Power at work in ourselves and in the universe and "IT" works mostly through human means and we can unite with IT.

Béatrice Walsh

www.ingramcontent.com/pod-product-compliance
Lightning Source LLC
LaVergne TN
LVHW010600070526
838199LV00063BA/5021